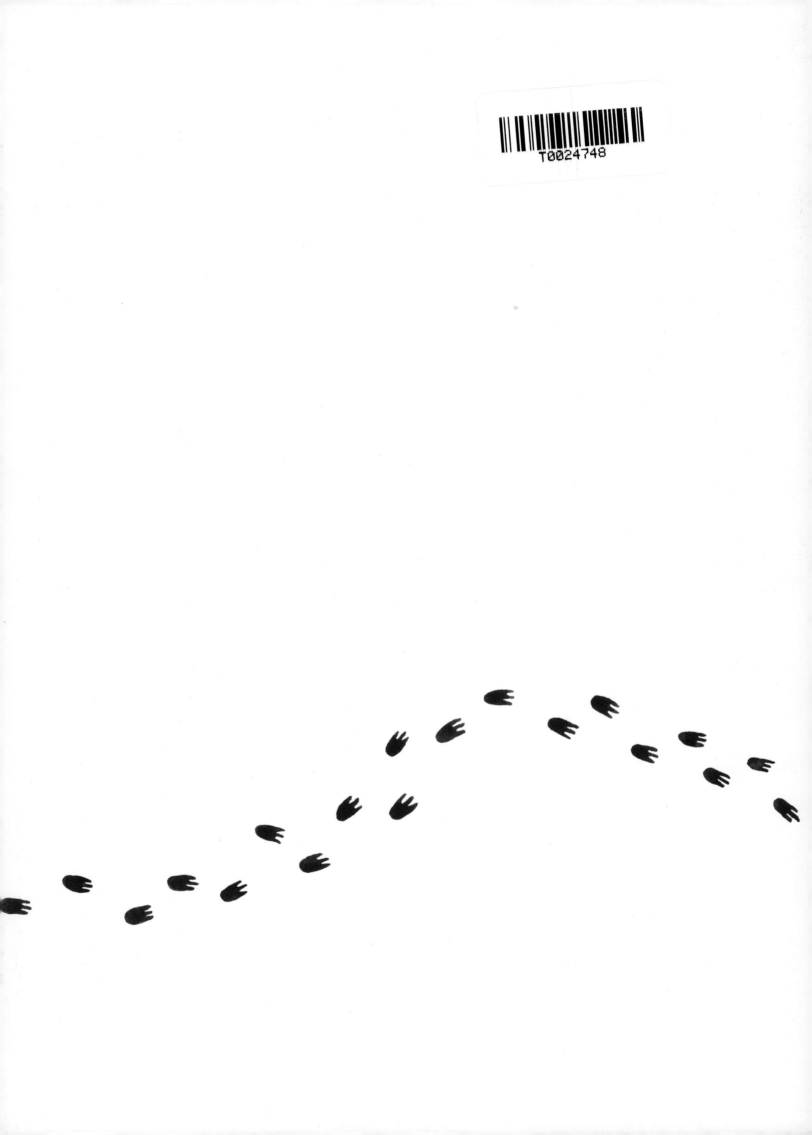

Little Mouse's Encyclopedia

Translation by Nick Frost and Catherine Ostiguy
Book design by Běžíliška
Proofreading by Nick Frost

Special thanks to Charlotte Parent and Marie Fradette.

This edition published in 2024 by Milky Way Picture Books,
an imprint of Comme des géants inc. Varennes, Quebec, Canada.

Library and Archives Canada cataloguing in publication
Title: Little Mouse's encyclopedia / text and illustrations, Tereza Vostradovská;
translation, Nick Frost, Catherine Ostiguy.
Other titles: Hravouka. English.
Names: Vostradovská, Tereza, author, illustrator. | Frost, Nick, translator. |
Ostiguy, Catherine, translator.
Description: Translation of: Hravouka.
Identifiers: Canadiana 20220014868 | ISBN 9781990252181 (hardcover)
Subjects: LCSH: Ecology—Juvenile literature. | LCSH: Nature—
Juvenile literature.
Classification: LCC QH541.14.V6713 2022 | DDC j577—dc23

ISBN: 978-1-990252-18-1
Printed and bound in China

Milky Way Picture Books
38 Sainte-Anne Street
Varennes, QC J3X 1R5
Canada

www.milkywaypicturebooks.com

Canada

We acknowledge the support of the Government of Canada.

Conseil des arts   Canada Council
du Canada   for the Arts

We gratefully acknowledge for their financial support of our publishing
program the Canada Council for the Arts and the Government of Canada.

LITTLE MOUSE'S ENCYCLOPEDIA

by Tereza Vostradovská

This is Little Mouse. She lives in a cozy burrow and
enjoys drinking tea, snacking on lemon cookies,
and reading encyclopedias.
She loves encyclopedias!

Because of them, she's learned that an altimeter
measures altitude, that a bathyscaphe is different
than a submarine, and how bicycle
gear systems work.

One day, while wrapped up in an article about
Earth's magnetic poles, a root suddenly pierces
the ceiling of her burrow. Whoops! Intrigued,
she decides to hang a lamp on it. But little
by little, more and more roots start to appear...

"Huh. Where are all these roots coming from?"
Little Mouse wonders. "And what will I tell
my aunties when they visit at the end of
the summer?

"If I observe what's happening around
my burrow, I can write down
my findings and draw little diagrams...
I know, I'll make my own encyclopedia!"

"Here's a great idea,"
she squeaks cheerfully!

Just like that, Little Mouse
heads out of her burrow.

AROUND
THE BURROW

As soon as Little Mouse steps outside, her first surprise awaits: even though each root is seemingly identical, they all come from different plants! Some round and elongated; some fluffy; and some that are different colors like pink, yellow, or blue...

⑤ ⑥ ⑦

Underground, our little mouse spots some white larvae. They look familiar to her, having seen some before in her aunt's pantry, but those ones were way smaller.

① ② ③ ④

1. Cetonia larva 2. Beetle larva 3. Millipede 4. Earthworm 5. Dandelion 6. Dead nettle 7. Fleabane 8. White clover
9. Common yarrow 10. Deptford pink

"Earthworms and larvae? Ew, no thanks!"

Further away, Little Mouse spots a burrow of sleeping shrews and catches a whiff of their dinner.

11. Cabbage white (or cabbage butterfly)   12. Thyme   13. Spotted knapweed   14. English plantain (or lance leaf plantain)
15. House centipede   16. Masked shrew

HOW TO MAKE A HERBARIUM

Back at her burrow, Little Mouse jots her findings down in a notebook. During her first expedition, she delicately compiled her favorite plants, which she's now using to start a collection of preserved plant specimens known as a "herbarium."

After removing the soil from each plant's roots, she slips the plants between two sheets of newspaper, then puts everything under a big pile of books. Once the plants are pressed and dried, Little Mouse will tape them to sheets of paper — and voilà!

1. Pick plants while the sun is shining.

2. Attach plants to a sheet of paper with sticky tape. Cover them with a second sheet of paper.

Required:

The flower
*
the stem
*
the leaves
*
and the roots.

VYNÁLEZY
MOŘE & OCEÁNY
CYKLISTIKA
LETECTVÍ

3. Place everything under a pile of books.

4. Worth noting:
Name: English plantain
(or lance leaf plantain)
Latin name: Plantago lanceolata
Date of picking: June 19, 2024

HOW TO CATCH INSECTS

Put a piece of meat,

a bit of vinegar,

and a slice of apple in a pot.

A pot

"How can I study insects and larvae?" Litte Mouse wonders. "I know, I can attract them with a piece of meat or fruit! But I don't want to stick them to paper like I did with the plants. Sometimes, insect specialists known as 'entomologists' put them to sleep and use pins to hold them in place. I prefer to release them after observing them."

"Don't forget to release them!"

"These larvae look very similar, yet they'll become very different insects."

1. Bellflower 2. Creeping buttercup 3. Grasshopper 4. Daisy (or white daisy) 5. Crane fly larva 6. Moth cocoon 7. Wireworm 8. Mole cricket
9. Sexton beetle larva

Little Mouse continues exploring.
At the side of the stream,
she's making new discoveries.

(10)
(11)
(14)
(15)
(16)
(12)
(13)
(17)

"Hey, I found earthworms!
These ones got bitten by a mole
so that they can't squirm away.
That way, they'll still be alive and
fresh when she eats them later.
Poor things! Nature can
be cruel sometimes!"

10. Forget-me-not   11. Gerris   12. Eastern newt   13. Caddis worm   14. Frog tadpole   15. Yellow marsh marigold   16. Purple loosestrife   17. Mole

THE FOOD CHAIN

"I saw larvae devouring the roots and found the mole's food reserves to be full of earthworms," Little Mouse recounts in her notebook. "I observed a water bug looking out for midges. I spotted tadpoles and newts eyeing up a water strider, just waiting to pounce on it. And I heard a marten over in the bush, who definitely wouldn't have turned its nose up at a well-fed mouse! High above the meadow, a buzzard flew in a circle, no doubt delighting over the marten and a mole."

"If I drew all of this in my notebook, I could show how the food chain works!"

What a treat!

Yum!

Grass grows using the sun's energy.

Certain small critters feed on grass, roots, and seeds.

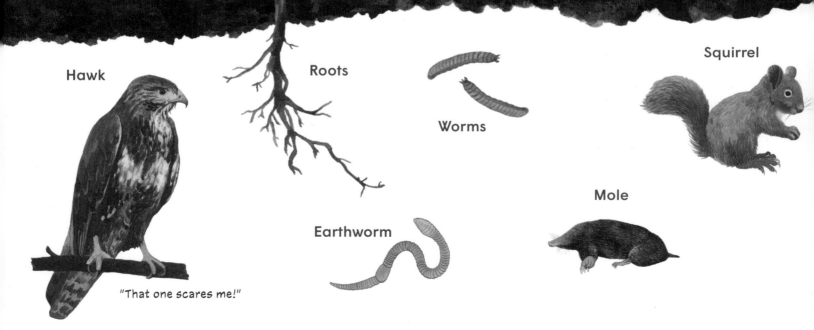

Hawk

Roots

Worms

Squirrel

Mole

Earthworm

"That one scares me!"

Hey, you know about the food chain?

No, why? Should I?

Larger animals eat smaller ones — and even sometimes eat other large ones!

The largest of all — whether they're a wild animal, a bird of prey, etc. — aren't a target because no animal hunts them.

Grass

"These are nine plants and animals. Can you figure out four different combinations of food chains among them?"

Hazelnuts

Marten

"I love hazelnuts!"

"That one scares me too!"

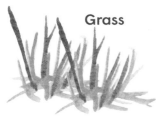

Hazelnut-mouse-hawk   Hazelnut-mole-hawk   Grass-worm-mole-marten-hawk   Roots-earthworm-mole-mole-marten-hawk   Hazelnut-squirrel-marten-hawk

THE
FOREST

A worn-out pine cone lies on the path, its scales everywhere. "What likely happened here is that a squirrel nibbled the seeds and left the rest," Little Mouse says. "If I look around, I might catch the little critter."

She picks her research back up the next day. The forest path is carpeted with thorns and moss. "It's so soft," she rejoices, stretching her legs.

1. Common wood-sorrel   2. North American red raspberry   3. Hawkmoth   4. American red squirrel   5. Pine   6. Blueberry   7. Bolete
8. Slug   9. Common June beetle

"Hee hee! What's tickling me...? Ah, it's the ants! I wonder what their role is in the forest..."

10. White pincushion moss   11. American badger   12. Spruce   13. Hairy woodpecker   14. Spider   15. Strawberry tree   16. Porcupine   17. Ant

ANTS AND OTHER DECOMPOSERS

In nature, even waste gets used. Earthworms, larvae, and insects feed on dead leaves or dead animals, allowing for decomposition to take place and soil to be enriched with nutrients needed for tree growth.

Little Mouse turns her focus to the ants. In her notebook, she remarks that the anthill she sees functions a bit like a small town. Worker ants run around searching for food, drops of water, and building materials. That's in addition to raising their larvae and eliminating any harmful insects they come across.

"I'm examining the field!"

Look over there! It's a larva!

An ant uses its mandible (jaw) as teeth, which are razor sharp — especially in guard ants.

Mushrooms (fungi) and insect larvae contribute to the decomposition of dead wood.

If you stare at the forest floor long enough, you'll definitely see ants.

Aphids produce a sweet liquid called "honeydew," which ants feed on.

Be careful: some ants sting! Only the queen lays eggs.

Perched on a branch, Little Mouse notices that each tree has different leaves. Some are flat, while others are thin and pointy like needles. In forests left undisturbed by humans, she can also see that these trees all have different ages. Older ones often serve as shelters for small animals and seedlings growing their bases.

"That weird little ball on the leaf is the gallnut. Who would suspect this is actually the home of an itty-bitty larva?"

"It was introduced by a parasite, the gall wasp, which bites the leaf to deposit it."

1. Oak gall 2. Weevil 3. Oak 4. Marten 5. Beech 6. Heather 7. Fly agaric

She goes in for a closer look: if the stump is hollow, it might be home to an anthill. Little Mouse, however, prefers not to disturb the snake, which is getting warm in the sun.

HOW DO TREES GROW?

Little Mouse takes some acorns out of her reserves and, rather than keeping them for dinner, plants them in the ground. An acorn is a seed, after all! In just a few weeks, roots will form and a small oak tree shoot will rise above the surface of the Earth.

She knows that the tree trunk will thicken over time. The wood grows under its bark in summer, then rests in winter. Each year, new layers of wood appear, forming growth rings, visible on stumps or fallen trees. "If I count them, I'll know the age of the tree."

Woo-hoo! A new oak tree!

The first leaves begin to develop...

and the plant grows.

The seed's outer layer bursts open underground.

After a few days, a tiny root appears.

This seedling is a small tree.

The tree's age

My age

The thickness of the growth rings depends on the amount of light, nutrients, and water the tree receives. A thick circle indicates a year of good climatic conditions, while a thin circle indicates a bad year — one with severe drought or lots of frost, for example. Sometimes, you can even see the growth rings on a piece of wooden furniture!

① ③ ⑦

② ④ ⑥ ⑤

Wow, what a heavy pine cone!

Little Mouse has collected some fruits and seeds. Do you know to which tree they belong?

1. Elm 2. Hazel 3. Beech 4. Maple 5. Alder 6. Lime 7. Fir

Little Mouse climbs a tree and notices with astonishment that, even up high, there's a lot of life to be found.

While watching the birds, she must be very attentive, as their plumages often blend in with the surrounding vegetation. This is especially common among females, as it allows them to take care of their younglings without drawing attention. Little Mouse is also surprised to discover a nest containing four eggs, three blue and one speckled. "How is that possible? It must be a cuckoo's egg," she remarks. "The speckled egg was laid in the nest of another bird to be incubated and fed."

1. Lichen (or usnea catfish)   2. Hylobius   3. Barred owl   4. Northern cardinal
5. Skater spider   6. Red-breasted nuthatch

An owl has built its nest in the hollow trunk of an old oak tree. The bird is only active at night, but Little Mouse doesn't wait around: since the owl is a carnivore, it might try to devour her.

In the forest, bees collect the honeydew produced by aphids because there are very few flowers. That's why forest honey is dark and has such a distinct taste.

7. Deer mouse 8. Wasp 9. Black-billed cuckoo 10. Hawk 11. Aphid 12. Blue jay 13. Bee 14. Mistletoe

BIRD SONGS

peek, peek, peek, peek

Hairy woodpecker

jeer, jeer

Blue jay

Early this morning, even before sunrise, Little Mouse wakes to the sound of birds singing. "What chaos! Why don't these birds sleep in?" she sighs.

coo-oo, coo, coo, coo

Mourning dove

fee-bee

Black-capped chickadee

caw, caw, caw

American crow

cheerily, cheer up, cheer up, cheerily, cheer up

American robin

what-cheer, what-cheer, what-cheer, whoit, whoit, whoit

tsee, tsee, tsee, tsee, tsee

Golden-crowned kinglet

chirrup, chirrup, chirrup

House sparrow

Northern cardinal

Too awake to fall back to sleep, she leaves her burrow and sits on a branch, notebook in hand, to jot down each bird's song.

BIRD FEATHERS

Nearby, a black-capped chickadee cleans its feathers. Little Mouse silently observes it, taking note of its three different types of feathers.

On its wings and tail, flight feathers allow it to soar.

Contour feathers protect it from rain and wind.

Down feathers cover the bird's skin, helping it maintain its temperature.

1

2

3

Little Mouse has found three pretty feathers. Do you know to which bird each of them corresponds?

1. Pheasant   2. Common buzzard   3. Blue jay

THE POND

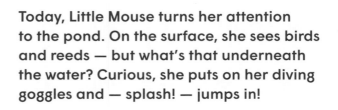

Today, Little Mouse turns her attention to the pond. On the surface, she sees birds and reeds — but what's that underneath the water? Curious, she puts on her diving goggles and — splash! — jumps in!

1. Great blue heron   2. Reed mace   3. Flowering rush   4. Great ramshorn   5. Muskrat   6. Pondweed   7. Nepa cinerea   8. Leech   9. Water lily

"Reeds make up their own type of forest, but with an underwater component. They're home to birds, insects, and amphibians. These animals hide between stems to escape predators who might otherwise easily hunt them," she muses.

Little Mouse notes with surprise that, underwater, life is very present! There are plenty of tadpoles and even more in the stream next to her burrow. "I still don't know when and how their hind legs grow," she thinks to herself, eager to solve this mystery.

10. Marsh wren   11. Reed grass   12. Clark's grebe   13. Dragonfly   14. Pike   15. Dragonfly larva   16. Swamp lymnaea

LIFE UNDERWATER AND IN THE MUD

To better understand how a tadpole develops, Little Mouse catches several of them with a net. After a bit of observation, she reaches a conclusion: "The frog lays its eggs and tiny tadpoles come out. As they grow, their hind legs appear and their tails shorten little by little. That's when the tadpoles become frogs!"

She then examines the pond floor. "The stems of dead reeds and grass, dead fish, and the excrement of ducks and other animals accumulates here at the bottom. All of these remains decompose and form the mud that various species live in, including certain insect larvae, crustaceans, bivalves, and many others. Mud contains essential nutrients for plant growth, so it's important for the pond to function properly."

Hey! Don't trap me!

Don't worry, I'll let you go after.

4

3

2

1

This is a nepa cinerea. It breathes with the help of this tube, which it uses like a snorkel.

The stripes on this shell indicate age, like a tree's growth rings.

I'm pretty old.

BREATHING UNDERWATER

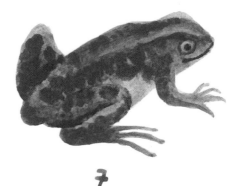

5

6

7

"When I swim underwater, I have to hold my breath, so I've always wondered how animals who live in the pond do it. It looks like it depends on the species. Fish, for example, absorb oxygen from the air that dissolves in water through their gills, which are right where my hands are." And just like that, Little Mouse quickly comes up for air.

The air trapped under my elytra allows me to float. If I want to dive, I have to swim rather hard.

Ribbit, ribbit...

Hello, I'm a seashell!

Little Mouse hasn't finished exploring the whole pond just yet, so she dives back in. "Maybe I'll find something unexpected," she thinks to herself.

She carefully cleans her diving goggles so they don't fog up and puts them on. Then she puts on her flippers, takes a deep breath, and jumps out of the boat.

"Ah, that's why ducks swim so easily! They have webbed feet a bit like me when I've got my flippers on."

1. Whorl-leaf watermilfoil   2. Seashell   3. Cristatella   4. Carp   5. Canada waterweed   6. Mosquito larva   7. Aquatic buttercup   8. Harris's sparrow

Little Mouse stands on a stick stuck in the bottom of the pond. "There are a lot of insects flying just above the surface, which means their larvae must be close. A small amount of water or swamp is usually enough for mosquitoes."

"Look, a water shrew! It lives underground like me, but hunts for its food underwater, like small fish and frogs."

9. Mosquito   10. Black duck   11. Backswimmer   12. Water shrew   13. Great diving beetle   14. Green frog   15. Water spider   16. Brown bullhead

MOVING AROUND UNDERWATER

From her many dives, Little Mouse has observed the multitude of ways animals move through water and how their morphologies help them adapt to aquatic life. For example, webbing — the membranes stretched between fingers — encourages the use of legs as fins. Ducks' large webbing helps them direct their movements in the water and support themselves on the surface when they take off or land. Similarly, the aquatic shrew, thanks to its own webbing, can swim or hunt insects or snails underwater. Diving beetles and water bugs also have enlarged legs.

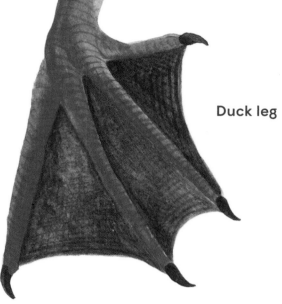

Duck leg

Fish scales partially overlap each other and improve swimming efficiency.

Frog leg

"I don't have fins, which is why I swim with flippers."

Shrew leg

STUDYING AQUATIC ORGANISMS

Using a sieve or a net, try to catch some animals. If you put them in a jar, don't let it sit in the sun. If the water gets too hot, they could die!

A jar filled with water

A net or a colander

If you find lots of animals and plants in the water, that means the pond is healthy.

A shallow bowl for sorting samples

THE GARDEN

Little Mouse takes a stroll through the orchard to take a look at the fruit trees, like this pear tree, which bear small, green fruit. "The pears will continue to grow and, by mid-August, will be sweet and as big as me," she imagines.

1. Swallowtail   2. American goldfinch   3. Thistle   4. Monarch butterfly   5. Rusty blackbird   6. Cedar waxwing   7. Pear tree   8. Black-capped chickadee

There are bees everywhere! In her notebook, Little Mouse writes: The bee lands on the flowers and drinks the sweet nectar, while their down catches the pollen.

The bee carries it from one flower to another. This is called "pollination" — the fertilized flowers will give out seeds that will germinate.

9. Earwig   10. Apple tree   11. Bee   12. Poppy   13. Nettle   14. Currant   15. Mourning dove   16. Plum tree

MAKING A POND IN THE GARDEN

Little Mouse decides to dig a pond for the animals in the garden. It'll be a place where birds cool off and butterflies come to drink on hot days, and where tadpoles and insect larvae can develop. "It'll be like a small swimming pool!" she rejoices. Animals need water to live. You, too, can set up a pond in your garden.

"A true oasis!"

Phew, such hard work!

1. First, dig a hole. Make a gentle slope for entry into the water.

2. Line it with a special film.

3. Place pebbles around the edge and fill the basin with water.

4. The animals will come all on their own.

In the vegetable garden, Little Mouse is surprised by the variety of fruits and veggies grown in such a small area. "Could I name all these plants?" she wonders. "I'll draw carrots and kohlrabi in my journal."

"This big caterpillar loves lettuce. I hope it leaves some for me!"

1. White admiral   2. Potato   3. Brown-lipped snail   4. Woodlouse   5. Radish   6. Lettuce   7. Large white caterpillar   8. Tomato   9. Onion   10. Garlic

"With tomatoes, we eat the fruit itself; with lettuce, we eat the leaves; cauliflower, we eat the flower. But with carrots, we eat the root. It's the roots that attract me, but I know that if I nibble on them, the plant won't be able to survive."

"I'll still eat this one. Look, a caterpillar has already taken a bite!"

11. Brussels sprouts 12. Kohlrabi 13. Ladybug (or ladybird) 14. Hamburg parsley 15. Carrot 16. Green June beetle 17. Pea 18. Cauliflower 19. Leek

FRUITS AND VEGETABLES

Picnic time! Little Mouse gathers up a few fruits and veggies to snack on. When she gets to the tomato, she wonders out loud, "is it a fruit or vegetable?" It's an interesting question and, oftentimes, when scientists try to differentiate fruits and vegetables, they don't always agree.

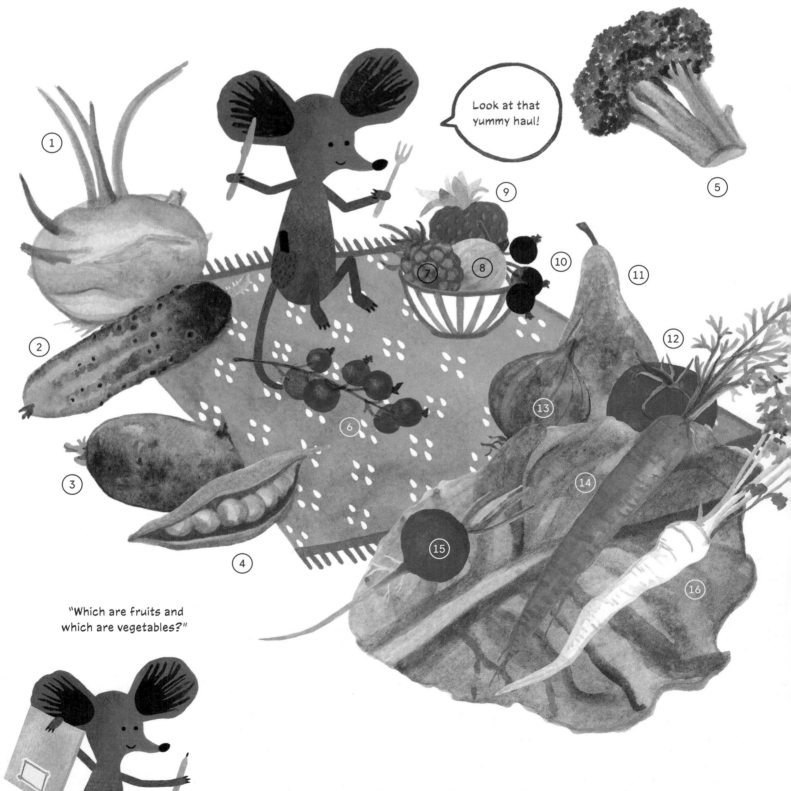

"Which are fruits and which are vegetables?"

Vegetables: 1. Kohlrabi 2. Pickle 3. Potato 4. Pea 5. Broccoli 13. Onion 14. Carrot 15. Radish 16. Hamburg parsley
Fruits: 6. Currant 7. Raspberry 8. Gooseberry 9. Strawberry 10. Blueberry 11. Pear 12. Tomato

GROWING AROMATIC PLANTS

While walking in the garden, Little Mouse spots a few strange plants, which, according to her, have a variety of delightful scents. "It's probably mint, chives, and parsley, which would be delicious in my cheese soup," she says, licking her lips.

She places the planter at her burrow's entrance so the plants have enough light to grow. "When they're big and strong enough, I'll replant them in the grass."

1. At the bottom of a planter, place small pebbles.

2. Put down soil so the plant doesn't stagnate in water and the roots don't rot on the stones.

3. Chives, mint, and parsley should be planted carefully.

4. Cover the roots with soil.

Mint

Chives

Parsley

Don't forget to water them!

Back in her burrow, Little Mouse works long and hard to finish up her nature encyclopedia. Her aunts' visit is approaching and she's very excited to show it to them!

Over the summer, she collected a myriad of samples, drawings, and information. "I still need to finish drawing all the fruit pits," she sighs, "and I can't forget the little caterpillar that nibbled the lettuce leaves... Oof, I need to tidy up too."

Leaves

Root

"Everything is a mess; I can't find anything!"

Did you know?
This book was also made into a fun video game
and interactive encyclopedia available in
18 different languages!

If you're as curious about nature as I am,
check out **Little Mouse's Encyclopedia**,
available for Nintendo Switch, Xbox One,
PlayStation 4, iPhone, and Android!